To My Dearest
Lance
What more (
Thank You

MW01109612

Manners Over Money

To Get the Money, You Need the Power!
To Keep the Power, You Need the Respect!

Shannon "Lady Tiunna" Morris

Manners Over Money

ISBN 978-1726410922

"Like a therapist, or the local barkeep, hairdressers are in a position of trust. We are transforming not just how a person looks but how they feel..."

-Tabatha Coffey

DEDICATION

I dedicate this book to Lee Moss,
Miss Yvonne, and my Mommy.
Thank you for giving me a great foundation to build on.

Acknowledgments

"**You can only become truly accomplished at something you love. Don't make money your only goal. Instead, pursue the things you love doing, and then do them so well that people can't take their eyes off you.**"

-**Maya Angelou**

From the time I was a baby, all through elementary school, I was called ugly. Not that you have an ugly attitude ugly, like you're nice and cool, but you're physically ugly. Kids used to tease me until I cried myself home. Walking through the neighborhood filled with anger, sadness, rejection, self-doubt, snot and tears. Wonders, why? I can't help that I have this short nappy unmanageable mind of its own type of wild hair. I can't help that my teeth are as big as a rabbits teeth, with a gap so big that kids literally think I'm missing a tooth. My skin is scaly as an alligator and I have the body of a boy child. Mind you, kids were developing, but not me.

My mom used to try her best to keep me looking nice. She struggled with me and keeping me together all the time. I was her wild child...her messy kid...her kid that tore up everything she had...borrowed or wore...especially my hair. My hair was ALWAYS the struggle. She had tried everything with my hair. She used to press it with this Hot Comb you put on top of the stove and let the fire warm it up to straighten your hair. I used to cry before she would even get started. Man, I don't know why we always sabotage ourselves. I had totally freaked myself out being scared. It's like sitting around waiting for something negative to happen, and you know what, it did and I brought it upon myself.

I already knew I was going to get burned by that Hot Comb, especially since the edges of my hair were SO short. The process of putting that hair grease on my hair, then putting that HOT comb to my hair to straighten it, hearing that grease sizzle and popping on the Hot Comb was enough to make me flinch, and the IT happens. I get burned! Of course my mom always said "well if you be still" shaking my head, I'm like, "you burned me" and she would be like "girl turn around that was the was the heat from the grease." That was the worst for me.

Then, the natural braid styles came out... you know when they were called "Pinch Braids" now they call then Pixies. I was so happy to be getting away from that Hot Comb honey, but didn't realize that all this beauty comes with a price. I remember the first time my mom was setting up to braid my hair. I walked into the Living Room area of the house and saw bags and bags and I do mean BAGS of hair. I'm not joking, it was like 12 bags oh this Synthetic SUPER long hair. I remember thinking to myself "WOW, what is all that for?" None the less I was just happy I didn't have to worry about getting burned, so I was happy.

Well, my happiness did not last very long. Once my mom started braiding my hair (which was pulling my eyes and brain so tight, it still kind of burned) I soon learned that it would take 12 hours to install hundreds of these braids. OMG NO! Then, "Dookie Braids" came out, which were the same as Pinch Braids but bigger, now called Box or Goddess Braids. These weren't so bad, since they didn't take as long, still painful, but I liked these better. Especially, since they had these gold balls that I could clip onto the ends of my braids for decorations.

Yeah, I used to LOVE these. Oh, baby but wait what about...the Jheri Curl. This hairstyle was like a love/ hate relationship. I used to love this look, but of course the process was tedious. The smell of these chemicals would have the entire house stinking, but the best part was when my mom would do the Cold-Water Rinse, to seal the curls in. I knew that was the last part of the process, before I got to put all my Activator and Moisturizer in my hair, and put the plastic cap on to hold the moisture in. I mean we used to walk around the neighborhood with these plastic caps on. We were so serious about keeping out Jerri Curl juiced up. Moisture was and still is the key to hair growth.

Oh yeah, you couldn't tell me nothing with that. It was like having naturally curly hair, until it dried out...lol. Then the "Perms" hit ... (Relaxers) this is a Straightening Systems. This was my favorite procedure. Although it felt cold and slimy, it was short and sweet. Once I learned that it only burns if you scratch your scalp the day you are getting it done, I started, beating myself in the head. Come on now, you know the "pat your weave" technique...lol. I swear my scalp only started itching, when it knew it was getting a Relaxer that day. So it seemed. See how your mind can play tricks on you? You have more control than you give yourself credit.

By the time 5th grade hit, my mom had had enough of my hair and took me to the salon she went to regularly. That's when I met the lady that would change my life forever. I walked into the salon for the first time as a client. Now I had been there with my mother before, but never as a client. I will never forget this. I walked in for my appointment and the Hairstylist that my mom goes to, was waiting for me. Little ole ugly nappy headed me. And you know what? She was happy to see me. It showed. She was smiling, she was pretty, dressed well, smelled good, hair was laid, and she was excited about giving me my new look. She was

PRETTY. She was POISE and she was POLITE. I knew I was about to be pretty.

That's all I wanted. She LAID. My. Hair. OUT! This hairstylist had me feeling like never before. I was so happy and proud to be me for the first time in a VERY long time. I felt pretty. I felt happy. I felt like showing off. I felt like turning around in circles jumping up and down with happy joy. It felt good! I decided then that that's all I wanted to be when I grew up... to be pretty and make people happy. This lady and her manners (Customer Service) had totally altered my insecure thoughts. That's so powerful I thought. Like, WOW, what an amazing lifestyle. This lady has to not only make people beautiful on the outside, but beautiful on the inside as well. That's when I decided I wanted to be a hairstylist.

Table of Contents

Introduction

When I decided to write this book, I thought about my son Luke. I wanted him to know the importance of how to treat people. I wanted him to know about mannerism, and about how you are perceived by people from when they first lay eyes on you. It is very important to me that I teach him what's in a solid foundation....

RESPECT! SELF-RESPECT! It is so very important for me to give him a good foundation to build on. Oh yes! That starts with self.... oh, and you won't get far without respect. So, Self-Respect is where you need to begin I thought. When I was growing up, the neighborhoods were MUCH different than they are now. Now days there aren't very much "neighborly" things happening in the hood. Yes, now it's just a lot of "hoods." Strangers, living next door to strangers. I never understood how you could be living next door to someone and they are living a secret life. I'm sorry, but I'm that friendly, inviting, how are you doing, I may have pulled your trash can out to the curb if you forgot, and trimmed your grass with mines, type of neighbor. I mean shoot we us used to know our neighbors. It was actually safe to walk the neighborhood and go inside your friend's house.

Yes, friend I said Friend, because that's exactly what we had then. Friends. Friendships. I mean we knew each other's last names, we played at each other's houses, and if you got too grown or disrespectful? Honey please. The neighborhood could actually put you on a punishment. (It was like "Adult Alliances" back then ...sheesh). Those punishments used to be crucial. Sometimes you would much rather just take a whooping and have it over with, then it's like all the parents got hip to that a switched it up on us kids and went for the torture.

PUNISHMENTS! Not that I'm going to take your game away punishment...since back then gaming systems were rare and you had to share them with your siblings. That wasn't the punishment. The punishment was you cannot come out your room FOR ANYTHING, but to use the rest room and get water. And don't be too thirsty trying to be out that room because my momma was NOT having that. She got hip QUICK.

I remember I was at my Best Friend's house playing Double Dutch. Because you know back in the day to be outside was where it was at. You were either walking to the neighborhood   park that everyone would be hanging out at. OOH, I remember the basketball court used to be SO PACKED ...or walking to the neighborhood gas station (multiple times a day sometimes). This was fun to us. Visiting a friend's house and playing in the creek, Man, the creek used to run through the neighborhood all the way to our elementary school. We would find all kinds of frogs and turtle, while splashing around in that creek water, jumping and skipping rocks.

We were so fearless of the living things in this creek. Wait, we used to build these club houses in between the houses in the neighborhood and not necessarily our house, we just needed a good spot with lots of trees, and if this were your house, well sorry, there will be kids living on your property...well, once we built our little cardboard and sheet house....lol. The neighbors never minded this, because it was all so innocent. Yeah, the good ole days. Being outside, making up dance routines at you friend's house and jumping Double Dutch. I was so good at Double Dutch. My mom was cold though. She had taught so many of the neighborhood kids how to jump. So, you know I was cold.

Man, I was at my BFF's house jumping one day and when it was my turn to jump, the friends turning were turning "claps". That's what you called it when the ropes aren't being properly turned, and that's serious. I could hear that it was wrong, see, if they were turning correctly I would hear,,, tap, tap, tap, tap. But, that's not what I heard. I heard tap tap, tap tap, tap tap. OH NO! I thought to myself, and I had convinced myself (within seconds cause when you defensive it happens that fast) that they (my friends) were doing this on purpose. Man, I must have gotten so mad, and I started cussing those girls (now they not my friends of course…smh) that were turning those clapped ropes, OUT honey.

Man, I was on a roll too like a grown up. I don't even know why I would be talking to my friends like this. I knew I was wrong. I mean I loved my friends. So, why would I get so mad that I would sabotage myself?! See, I let my emotions get the best of me and lost my self-respect, which made me lose self-control. That sent me to being disrespectful, which only led to disaster…trouble. And I knew this, but when you are mad you don't care, right? Wrong, there is no pause button, but there should be. Then I heard my friend's mom call saying, "Shannon telephone." I was like omg. This is cool. Who is calling me from here? I thought I was all that because a kid getting a phone call at someone else's house was dope. Petty huh? I know, but back in the day, kids used to be so easy to satisfy. My, how times have changed.

Anyhow…I get to the telephone, all smiling, thinking I'm the stuff, and I hear "so you over there cussing?" It was my mom! This BF's momma got to be kidding me. She had called my mom and told her what I was doing. My mom told me to come home right now because she had something for me. The way she said it, I knew it wasn't anything good. I knew I was in BIG trouble then. My BF's mom ratted me out.

I was so mad at her that I rolled my eyes, even though I highly respected this woman. I thought, "WOW really how petty can you be?" I guess you can say she was like a second mom to me. I mean I was at her house every day, she bought me clothes, cooked me food and let me be in the house even when she wasn't there. My friend and I were so close she even let me spend the night on school nights since we went to the same school. That may not be a big thing to you, but back in the day, that just was unheard of. Shoot, kids were not allowed to be inside the house if the parents weren't there. And most parents just wouldn't let you have inside company AT ALL. That was my mom. She used to tell us you can have all the company you want...outside.

But when you knew your parents were on the way home, you had better start clearing off that front porch. Do as you will in the backyard. No one wanted to be in the backyard where no one can see you. All the action was on the front porch. Oh, and HECK NO, your friends can't come in, not even to use the bathroom. Parents knew that was the Sneak Attack to now look around, see your room, see their room, get some Kool-Aid and a snack. So, you know what? Use it outside. Oh yes, Boys and Girls. I knew one thing, when my mom was on her way home, I had better cleared camp. Meaning, even the outside company had better be gone. It had better not be any kids on her porch, in her backyard, or blocking her driveway. Respect.

Don't you hate it when you come home from a long day and some-one is blocking your parking space, or the stairs to your doorway, and they see you coming and still not move? You expect them to move and park their car in a more appropriate place. You want that respect, right. Same thing. Plus, we had to check in, once she was home. You know, for her to make sure we covered our daily chores and then we could go back outside. SHEESH my mom was so intimidating. Very nice, well mannered, soft spoken, pretty lady, that had no tolerance for bad excuse making kids. Like period. But, of course I always had a reason why something wasn't what it was supposed to be. Knowing I was wrong. It is hard to admit to yourself that you are the reason for where you are in life.

What kind of mark will you leave on this earth once you have left this land? I always tell my son, "Luke, people talk. And it's been proven that most of the time bad news spreads faster and lingers longer than good news." Now, ain't that a trip. What happened to "the 80/20 rule?" Where did "Your good outweighs your bad go?" I mean seriously, sometimes it doesn't matter how much good you do. You do one wrong thing. And that's what people tend to judge you on. Sad, but true.

That's why using something so simple as Good Manners is always appreciated. I always tell my son, "good manners can take you places money can't." Now, I know it takes money to make the world go around, but without good manners, you will not have the best opportunities to even get to the money. As a Licensed Cosmetologist for over 13 years, one thing that has never and will never change.... is GOOD CUSTOMER SERVICE...MANNERS, if you will? In this book you will ride the beauty industry wave with me and see how powerful manners can truly be. Bringing you so much peace, lasting relationships, respect, security, self-assurance and MO MONEY MO MONEY MO MONEY! Ready? Let's get booking.

You Better Check Yourself

"Good manners are just a way of showing other people that we have respect for them."

-Bill Kelly

Chapter 1

This book is necessary! I am SICK OF IT....it has to stop! I got to do something about these people and their poor Salon Etiquette. What happened to good manners, chivalry, sharing and caring and all the goodies in making another person feel good? Damn, I mean I know that we were raised from little bitty kids, to do what, "Mind our manners."

Now, I know you have heard this, your entire life. I'm sure you still tell this to people right now today. It seems to me that some adults feel that "minding your manners" is only for kids. (You know that saying your parents always pulled out on you. "Stay in a child's place" they would say. And you're like, "Well, grownups have a place too." But you better not DARE let those words roll out of your mouth, or BAM right in the lip. Old school whooping style. LBVS.).

FUNNY TRUE STORY: Back in the day my mom used to have all these little mini lipstick samples from a company she used to order makeup and costume jewelry from. I used to sneak in her makeup bag and take her sample lipsticks and pass them out to my friends. Yes, I know I had no business in my Mom's room, especially in her makeup.

But, I didn't care, once again that was a risk I was willing to take. Knowing it was wrong and knowing it could lead to disaster, but the temptation of being the cool girl and accepted all because of something so dangerously simple as taking Mom's Lipstick. I did it anyway. Well, one day I tried on my Mom's cute Red Lipstick she loved and wore almost every day.

When my mom pulled up I was waiting for her in the driveway, all excited. to show her how cute I looked, like she did, and you know what happened...BAM! My mom popped me right in my lips. For one, stealing out of her stash, like kids don't think their wrong plan all the way through, cause where else would I have gotten this lipstick. Uh Duh little girl you busted and you wrong and "I got something for you." Two having her lipstick on like I was grown, she didn't care I admired her and wanted to be her, all she saw was RED, and three, my friends had not cleared out yet, so yeah, they witnessed this public beat down. My mom made me go wash that lipstick that was now smudged (from that smack down) OFF and sent me right back outside.

Now you know I did not want to go back outside cause I was TOO embarrassed but there was no staying in the house option. Parents are smart like that. I guess that was the other part of my punishment, so I just moseyed my Big Lip self, back outside, just to get clowned (laughed at) by my friends. Well, we live and we learn. I surely didn't let her catch me in anymore of her makeup, but I was still smuggling little lipstick samples for me and my friends.....annnnnnnd...end scene lol.

This Manners Over Money method I have decided to live by comes from working in a salon and dealing with adults on a regular basis, up close and personal. I'm going to need these adults to practice what they preach and USE THEIR MANNERS...especially when they come into the salon to get a service.

I want everyone to have a reality check. I want you to be able to relate and see yourself in this book. I know we all have our opinions on how we would run another person's business. Well, when you are a part of that business, make sure you know how to run yourself first. We all know it is much faster and easier to just be blunt...short and straight to the point sometimes. I mean TIME IS SO VERY PRECIOUS. It's the only one thing you cannot get back. But, let's not be rude.

What happened to having a little finesse? Smooth talking has always worked. I like to drip my clients in it. When a person is spending their hard-earned money and quality time with you, it's nice to woo them a bit. Let them know that you really appreciate them for spending this time with you. Keep them in that good mood. You can sometimes tell a person's mood by their tone, posture, even the pace that they are talking.

You ever get into a heated discussion, not an argument, but the conversation is so good, you get all excited trying to make your point, and as you get closer to making your point, you start to speak faster and faster.... more aggressively? Yeah, we all have been here.

Well, that excitement can totally change your delivery. Being short, talking loudly, or fast paced can all be offensive and rude. What happened to treating people the way you want to be treated? I know you think people don't care and are so self-absorbed that they won't appreciate this. But, you will be surprised how the phrase "kill them with kindness" really does work. This can totally change your LIFE. Try it on today. Try it EVERY DAMN DAY! See how that makes you feel. I found that the best way to make yourself feel good is to share your good feeling with other people. Especially, strangers, or what about that person that you know who is usually in a bad mood for their own personal reasons, which has nothing to do with you, but they try to steer that negative energy in your direction? Just kill them with kindness. It's most satisfying, and it works.

Now, I know this sounds corny and WAY easier than doing. Deciding to use your "Manners Over Money' strategy can be a LIFE CHANGING experience, taking your clientele (your money), your relationships, and especially your LIFE for that matter, to another level. I read in Forbes Magazine that read to " treat people like people and not numbers, because people buy good feelings." Once I read that, my outlook on life and business, and how I treat people totally changed. I knew that people can get a good service anywhere, but once I learned that they were buying and coming back to me because of the way I made them FEEL and not just how they looked.... OH BOY!...that was a whole another ballpark.

Oh YES! I started practicing this "Manners Over Money" (I like to call it) technique, in a lot of my everyday encounters. Turns out, using good manners actually works. GO FIGURE! So, you mean to tell me all this time that I am in control of my happiness and most situations in my life? Absolutely, no one can take your happiness away but you. It's up to you. So, why give someone else your control? Be secure. Be sure. Be polite. Think first before you respond and react. Remember cause and effect.   One bad decision is like a rice grain in a puddle of water. There is always that ripple effect.

TRUE STORY....Stay With It!

10

I was taking a Color Class one day and left home thinking two things. #1 I want to see what this new color line was all about (because furthering your education means growth for you and your future endeavors). #2 I want a job opportunity with this company. Okay, so the night before, I prepped. I twisted my hair and got out business casual clothes and double checked my resume. I was ready! Woke up the next morning, got ready (showered, put on my favorite perfume, did my makeup, self-speech). You know the old "you know who you are, OWN IT, have a good dad, let's GET IT" speech. I was READY! I got in the car and noticed a stain on my coat, took that off and spilled coffee on my shirt! WHAT THE?! You know how at first you be so early for what you have to do, so you start to lollygag (wasting time) then you end up late, yeah that was happening. On top of that I had forgotten my resume. SHEESH I thought to myself, this is a disaster! So, I could have totally let this put me in a bad place, but why sabotage myself even more? I thought to myself, calm down and think.

Then, I saw a store, stopped there and bought a new shirt (ole trusty black is always easy). I changed in the car (desperate times calls for desperate measures) and headed to the class. I arrived! I wrapped my scarf around my neck, because, it was cold this day and my coat...well...yeah. Anyway, I headed into the class (15 minutes late), but the way I walked in you would have thought I was early. Nervous and all, but I had to put my GAME FACE ON. I walked through the door smiling, with the most welcoming spirit, walking, gracefully through the crowd, with the most enduring "excuse me" and "thank yous". (laughs in my own head cause I know I'm wrong as all out), but very serious. See, my kindness (mannerism) put the people (I was walking all over and in front of, blocking their view that they have paid good money for, to learn on their day off) at ease. I walked past one of my coworkers that was already there, and she whispered to me "you look pretty, all bright and vibrant." POWER! That made me smile, because that was exactly what I was going for, and I had on black.

Of course, I thanked her and returned the compliment. I immediately sat down, whipped out my iPad, and got down to business. In the middle of class they took a little break and passed out these survey sheets, asking what type of classes would we like to see in the future with this company? I noticed there was no, Customer Service or Relationship Building classes. I mean, without clients you have no business, so I added it. The owner of the store came around collecting the surveys and noticed my Salon Etiquette note and said. "Wow, now that's something that's not talked about." So I put myself out there saying I would love to come and talk to your class about that. Now, I was selling myself. Needless to say, he thought it was a great idea, so I left with a great job opportunity, just like I had planned. MONEY!

Toward the end of class one of the Hair models came up to me and asked what I used in my hair because she LOVED it and was looking for some different products for her natural hair as well. Now, this class was full of Licensed Cosmetologist, as she was, so this was very flattering to me. RESPECT! See, if another hairstylist comes up to you for hair tips, that's MAJOR! Well, to me at least. We began talking she said I was beautiful and had a welcoming sprit and that I should think about public speaking. See, making a good impression goes a long way. They key is to stay positive and in control of yourself. The deals are there. No matter what your case may be, when it comes to building something it all starts with the same foundation. YOU! If you have cracks in your foundation things are soon to come crumbling down.

HALF PRICE BOOKS.

EST. 1972

Half Price Books #123
630 N McKnight Rd
St Louis MO 63132-4911
314-991-6793

16-23 6:33 PM
re #0123 / Cashier DRob120 / Reg 2
e # 230785

SALE TRANSACTION

Business Traveler's Surv 3494220110	
2.00	$2.00
ct Mail for Dummies (Inf 2899774620	
3.00	$3.00
ers Over Money: To Get t 350481928U	
2.00	$2.00
zine mg	
1.00	$8.00

tems in Transaction

otal	$15.00
s Tax (9.238% on $15.00)	$1.39
-	$16.39

NT TYPE
2080 $16.39

s for shopping at Half Price Books!

H 0 2 0 1 2 3 0 0 2 2 3 0 7 8 5 9

HALF PRICE BOOKS

YOUR FAVORITE LOCAL BOOKSTORE. EVERYWHERE.

WHEN OUR STORES ARE CLOSED
JUST OPEN YOUR BROWSER.
SHOP HPB.COM FOR MILLIONS
MORE TREASURES ONLINE.

JOIN THE HPB EMAIL LIST AT
HPB.COM/JOIN & GET A
10% OFF COUPON TO SAVE ON
YOUR NEXT PURCHASE IN STOR

STORE RETURN POLICY

Cash refunds and charge card credits on all merchandise ar
available within 7 days of purchase with receipt. Merchandis
charged to a credit card will be credited to your account.
Exchange or store credit only for returns made with a gift rece
within 30 days of purchase date. Exchange or store credit w
be issued for merchandise returned within 30 days with rece
Cash refunds for purchases made by check are available afte
business days, and are then subject to the time limitations sto
above. Please include original packaging and price tag whe
making a return. Proper I.D. and phone number may be requi
where permitted. We reserve the right to limit or decline refur

Gift cards cannot be returned for cash, except as required by

The personal information you provide is confidential and v
not be sold, rented or disclosed to a third party for commer
or other purposes, except as may be required by law.

Are You Ready For The World

Life's most persistent and urgent question is, "What are you doing for others?"

-Martin Luther King, Jr.

Chapter 2

You want people to gravitate to you? You have more control over the opportunity if the person walks up to you. And the goal is to get long term power over a short-term victory, right? So, you need to be ready. Are you ready? Ready, to change, some lives? Ready, to get the deal, seal the deal, and secure the deal? Rather you are going on a job interview, scouting or being scouted, going to a dinner party, making public appearances, or just hanging out. You want to make your presence known. You want people to gravitate to you. Well, it starts with you.

Sure, it does. When you're in the type of business I am in.... THE BEAUTY INDUSTRY, it can be pretty tough. Classify a person as pretty and you automatically assume that they are pleasant. As a beauty provider I FEEL it is necessary to LOOK the part. Shit, live it. Enjoy it. I look at life as everyday being an opportunity to meet a new clients and build long lasting relationships. Once you walk outside your door, you are practically at work.

Good looks and good manners go a loooonng way. Try it and watch how people began to just gravitate to you. I like to tell myself these three things as I prepare myself for the outside world.

#1 Be Pretty.... it's just good manners I like to tease. LBVS (laughing but very serious)

#2 Have Poise... it's quite intriguing, make people want to get to know you and…

#3 Be Pleasant...it makes people come back for more of that feeling. ·

So, how do you get ready for the outside world? When you present yourself, how you look is usually how people are going to preserve you, especially strangers. All one has to go off at first is what the eyes see, and the prejudging starts there. Innocently! I always tease my friends, saying that people should want to look like me. LOL. I know that sounds really vein, but I mean nothing of the sort. What I'm saying is that people should admire you, your brand, and what you represent. Make yourself irresistible. Now, I'm not saying walk around with your chest puffed out, but if you are in the business of marketing, then, deep down inside, people should want to be you, or at least look as together as you. So, you need to have a trusting look about yourself. So, you need to be ON POINT.

I was in the salon one day...ear hustling...eavesdropping...listening in on someone conversation. I'm innocent though...lol. I heard a client telling her stylist she "cannot stand a hairstylist that doesn't keep her hair done and looks all thrown together." Which seems to be happening more often than it should! She then made a joke saying, "what if part of a client's payment went by according to how the stylist looked?" I piped in that conversation and said, "oh you mean like a sliding scale?" Now, what if, just WHAT IF, that, were the case? It would be like taking a test every day. Wouldn't it? Would you pass? Now you know we not ready for all of that, but you should be.

See, people have to get past what they see, before they can even get to the skills or give you a chance. Let's just go down a little list and check off what you did and did not do today and see if you think you passed. First, let me tell you that this is a test where you cannot miss, not a one. So, you need to be at 100%.

QUESTION...Lets be petty. 1. Did you iron those wrinkles out of your clothes? I know this sounds childish, but just because you are "only going to work...store...running errand etc." Did that mean don't care about the wrinkles, stained and holes? Aw, ok. When you get ready to impress and step on the scene rather it be a club an interview, a date, court, whatever. You make sure you are looking and feeling the part because you want the other persons to respect you. 2. Well, did you comb your hair? The biggest pet peeve people have with a hairstylist is they hardly have their own hair done. Like seriously though, who wants a barber with a bad haircut?! I know I don't. Now, let's dig a little deeper. Internal! 3. Did you tell yourself to have a good day? Seriously, did you? I mean, you are going to be telling this to people all day. Even strangers! So, why not start with yourself? I know this sounds corny but if you say this to others to make them feel good, why wouldn't you start with you? So, did you pass?

"Nobody trumps you" I like to tell my friends. It may sound selfish, but if you are not right, then you won't be right to help the people you love. I know I like to pump myself up every day. So, get your mind right for the outside world. Sit up straight, have good hygiene, as well as good energy you give off. Once I'm dressed, smelling good, feeling good, and looking good, I stop by my full body length mirror...(which everyone should have one of these, it does wonders for your self-esteem) lean my head to one side, tell myself "ooh you look pretty," take a couple selfies, and tell myself, "okay let's have a good productive day. LET'S GET IT."

It's gotten to the point that when my sister would hear me say these things...to myself and answer myself back (and no I'm not crazy...ok maybe a little, but a little crazy is good...lol) she would totally turn into a cheerleader. I practice the 3Ps (pretty, poise, and polite) because it has been proven to work. The combination of these three, really seem to put people at ease. Now, be just one or two and this can totally turn someone off. Presence is EVERYTHING.

FUNNY TRUE STORY: My sister Shai and her good friend taught me how to walk. No, for real, they taught me how to walk like a real lady. See, my sister's friend was older than us and way more experienced at being a woman. So, the two were NECESSRRY if I wanted to get this lady thing down pat. You now it takes a village honey...lol.

See, my sister always had such a strong straight back and good broad shoulders. She has such good posture to me. And people can tell a lot about you through body language. (BODY LANGUAGE: the process of communicating non-verbally through conscious or unconscious gestures and movement.) My sister to this day always shows confidence, assurance and pride. She would always get all the stares and smiles and "How are you doing pretty lady?" whenever we went places.

She is well respected, and I wanted that, too. Studies show that posture can tell you a person's confidence level. Keep that back straight and strong and people take you serious but slouch over and watch people walk right past you. So, in high school my sister taught me the meaning of posture and what it stands for. How to, walk tall, and proud. I remember it like it was yesterday...lol. She put me in a pair of my mother's high heels. Now I could walk, jump rope, and run in these heels, but it wasn't always like a lady if you know what I mean. And of course, we did this while my mom was at work. My mom would have flipped and probably will once she reads this book...knowing that we were playing in her good shoes.

Why is it, every time somebody has a favorite something they always called it their "good" whatever? Anyway. I could have straight torn my momma's shoes up playing around though for real. That was a chance I was willing to take to become this necessary lady. I guess that's why my sister didn't let me practice in her shoes. I remember walking from one end of the apartment complex we were living at the time to the other end of the parking lot. Like, it was a fashion runway show. My sister and her friend coached me daily until I got it right. Please believe me when I tell you I can RIP a runway now. Truth be told, I walk better than my teachers...lol. They are going to roll their eyes when they read this part. They may even challenge me to a Walk OFF.

Next, we moved into facial expressions. I was told that I have what people call a "'resting bitch face." Totally unaware of this I was wondering why people always asked "what's wrong? Are you ok? "Smile" they would say. I'm like I'm happy, so I had to be aware of my facial expressions because I was coming off as unapproachable. Ummm and that's not good when I'm trying to build long term relationships.

What's the first thing that happens to you when meeting someone for the first time? You see their look. From head to toe you begin to examine them (Sneaking). You make all these judgments. Looking for, some sort of expression. And unless "it" (the connection) happens, then you start to make up your own perception of that person being preju-diced (pre-judging) them. Even going so far as convincing yourself of, who and how they are, and it stops there. But, if "IT" happens and they look back at you, here comes that window of opportunity. This is usually when the connection happens, depending on the "Lookie" .... LBVS (laughing but very serious). Let's play a game.

Opening Doors

"Fear of the unknown paralyzes us, but without change we won't grow."

-Tabatha Coffey

Chapter 3

Game on! This is a game I like to call LOOKER vs LOOKIE. They say, "eyes are the windows to our souls." How your eyes look into another's eyes shows confidence, interest and honesty. Now a hard stare can be offensive, so use your eyes wisely...lol. When you (The Looker) look at a person and they (The Lookie) look back at you, it's going to tell you what your next move is. One of two things are going to happen here. You (The Looker) are either what I like to call IN or OUT. Childish and simple it may seem but a connection or disconnect can happen that fast.

EXAMPLE #1

You...The Looker, look at someone you may want to build a relationship with, giving them a little smile of hello (body language talk through your facial expressions), and they (The Lookie) give you back a little smirk (a cold dry hi) as I like to call it. Then it (the connection) probably stops there. You're OUT!

EXAMPLE #2.

You (The Looker) smile at someone you are interested in making a connection with. This time, The Lookie gives you back a smile and throws in a head nod (assurance). Not only is this warm and welcoming, the head nod assures you it is ok to engage and opens the door for conversation. Great! You're IN. You're IT. You're TURN!

Yes, it's that simple. Now what's your next move going to be? Let's talk about opening doors and keeping that door ajar for more opportunities. I mean that's what it's all about, right? We want to build long, lasting, relationships. No one WANTS to be a one hit wonder unless that's their thing. But I'm like a contractor of people honey. I like to build.

EXAMPLE:

Let's say you're in the beauty business. You walk into a store. Let's do a clothing store since I love to shop. You walk into the store. The person running the store greets you. "Hi. Thank you for coming in today. Is there anything I can help you find?" You smile and say, "No thank you, just, looking." Ok. So far so good you think to yourself. Okay they are greeting people and not harassing them and not following me all around the store. Ok. They are doing their job. (Inside conversation about their customer service being on point). So, you smile and are comfortable enough to stay in the store and continue to look around. While you're looking around another shopper notices you and tells you that you look pretty. What do you do?

A. Say Thank You and continue shopping

B. Say Thank You and return a compliment as well

C. Smile and say Thank You

Now, all of these are right. But, if you want to build a relationship, then I would have to go with B. For a total stranger to tell you that you look pretty. SHEESH. OH MY GOSH! That's something. I don't take that sort of thing lightly, especially when that's what I was going for. So, it is nice to be recognized. See this person has been checking you out; watching you; and they are intrigued by you. They already like something about you, so your next move should be easy. Your window is open. Let those curtains flow. See, I'm going to compliment you back, preferably your hair, because that's the business I am in.

If you're in the clothing business, then you would return a compliment about their clothes and so on, even if you don't really mean it. I know that sounds bad, but it does open that door. I'm going to engage in conversation. Yes. Right there at the store in line if need be. You have to do what it takes sometimes to keep your chair spinning or those curtains blowing...sort of speak. You have to look at every person you meet as a potential relationship; or someone they know could be a potential relationship. So be mindful of how you treat people, especially when you are not working because someone is always paying attention,

The Power of Presence....

Let's Get Cozy

Chapter 4

You walk into a salon for the first time and you get "the look." You know THEE LOOK. That ole side eye, who are you, what are you here for... (like that's not obvious) and who are you here for look. But, no one is saying anything to you. It's like as soon as you walked into the salon everyone stopped talking and started to stare at you. Ummmm, awkwarrrdddd. What's the deal with that anyway? Yeah, that would make anyone nervous and doubtful, including me. You're thinking, "Where is my greeting party because I know this ain't it." See, a more welcoming look, like a smile, (like the lady in the store from the last chapter) would have made this situation (the client) a little more comfortable.

This client came to you because they believe in you and your brand, and that's a good feeling. We (the salon as a whole including the clients) have to play a role in making sure we all get the look we are going for. The stylist and what location they choose plays a part. I mean you, are trusting, this location with your business as well. They teach you in Cosmetology School that the most important thing when starting a business is LOCATION. The client has to put total trust in the stylist and the people amongst them while they are sometimes isolated. You really have to keep a person relaxed, both adults and kids, so there is no clashing with anyone.

That's one of the reasons, location and atmosphere, are very important. But, isn't that why you (the hairstylist) chose to come to this location? It was something you liked about it. You trusted this location with your business. So, you expect your team to be just as accommodating as necessary. Meaning, if a client arrives before you (the stylist), then it's up to the salon team to welcome your client, keep them comfortable and check on them until their hairstylist arrives. This means treat them as if they are your client, take their name, let them know you are calling their stylist to see what the ETA (estimated time of arrival) is, and maybe even engage them into your conversation. This puts the waiting (possibly disturbed now that you're late) client at ease. And it gives the client a real understanding of how the salon operates as a whole (as a team, yet individually). I mean you have to cater to the clients because without them you really don't have a business. So, make sure your clients feel good from Hello! To, "See you next time!"

Here Is A Tip

It's always nice to be at the appointment time before your client gets there. I like to tease people and say "if you're on time then you're late, and if you're early then you are on time." Let your client walk in and see you there already waiting on them with a BIG smile that says, "HEY YOU!" Just watch the smile on their face when they walk through that door and see you already there! Greet your client by name (new clients love this). Make it so personable that it leaves such a good impression and makes them so comfortable. It may even increase your sale. As you are welcoming them, let them know you are excited about servicing them. Don't be too over the top or this can scare them. Keep, that good feeling going.

They came to you because they have total confidence in you and what you bring to the table. Once they are in your presence, it's up to you to keep that good feeling going. You now have to secure the deal.

So, be warm, welcoming, even quirky (even if you are just welcoming someone's else's client). In my experiences, I have found that being chipper and happy to see other's clients makes the clients so happy they will send business your way just for smiling and be welcoming.

You know what it's like to walk into a salon for the first time. So, you're already nervous (because your hair is all JACKED UP and you don't know who may be in there) so you kind of walk in timid and stiff. Even if you are a really confident person, the first time you meet someone (especially someone in the beauty industry), you can be a little intimidated. Even, if you know them. See, what you need to remember is that people are buying a good feeling. No matter what profession you are in.

So, just a regular ole service just won't do. Way before the client schedule with you, they have picked out the style (most of the time or they have some sort of idea of what they want) and that made them smile. They head nodded. Shoot, they even go so far as showing what they are thinking about getting to all their friends and family, asking them what they think. I mean they are really excited! They know just who to call, because this hairstylist be on point. You have to pull out all the stops. I mean, if you want to be one of THEE BEST in the game.

The reason why the client is confident in you is because from the first time they met you, you had such a strong, yet pleasant presence and they want some of that, or they saw some of your work and they had to experience your services for themselves. So, you have to pull out all the stops to make sure you don't deny them of that good feeling. Please believe that they are thinking, "Where is my welcoming party?" And you know what? That's just what they should get. I mean after all, they are spending their hard-earned money with you and that's an honor.

Shannon "Lady Tiunna" Morris

TRUE STORY

I worked with a young lady that was fresh into the field. She liked to wear bangled bracelets to work all the time. I mean, she did look so pretty coming into work. You could tell that she cared about her appearance. SELF RESPECT. But, I could also tell that her clients and others in the salon were irritated by the sound of her bracelets, especially, during their shampoo. If you didn't know, shampoos are what most clients are looking forward to during their service. I'm not going to lie, she did look really pretty and those bracelets were so cute.. (deep down inside I wanted them) POWERFUL! But, the sound was getting too annoying and alllll day. SHEESH!

So, one day I couldn't take it no more (and the owner of the salon never spoke on it until the girl wasn't in the room, then she would talk and tease). But as the owner I felt like it was her place to make sure the atmosphere stayed relaxing and fair. I couldn't take it no more! I yelled out "START A BAND WHY, DON'T YOU?!" I know. I know, totally unprofessional of me huh? I had totally lost myself. She had this look on her face (she was smiling though) but she was also like what's going on? She wasn't paying attention to the atmosphere, or her client. Maybe she doesn't know how to read facial expressions and body language, because there are many ways to talk without verbally speaking. (I know when your boss, mom, friend, husband, wife who ever) gives you a certain look, you usually know what they are trying to say.

My mom can still give me THE LOOK and I will mind my manners. Now I have mastered this too, I use it on my son...LOL. She was like aww my bracelets, what's the big deal, they are just bracelets. Well, to the person laid back trying to relax and a salon that has set the atmosphere of total relaxation, this was like a marching band. Needless to say she stopped wearing the bracelets to work but she also ended up quitting a couple months down the line.

Let's Talk About Setting The Atmosphere

"Like a therapist or the local barkeep, hairdressers are in a position of trust. We are transforming not just how a person looks but how they feel..."

-Tabatha Coffey

Chapter 5

You already know how people can get when it comes to their money. I know I don't play about mine. But money isn't everything; but it's necessary. Sometimes a client comes back for more of that good feeling you gave them. Because people buy good feelings; not just services. So, you want to set a nice relaxing atmosphere for your clients. Play some soft music. If you want the television on, then mute the sound. Why?

Well I found that as long as they can see the picture and read the captions, then that is entertainment enough for them. Plus, playing music low allows us to still have open discussions, while the television gives us something extra to talk about and the people under the dryer won't feel left out. When your client is going under the dryer, offer them a cold drink.... it's SUPER HOT under there, so make sure you try to keep them as cool and comfortable as possible, considering the HOT DRYER is the part that most people dread. So, WOOING (spoiling) right now is necessary (manners over money). "Love you CLIENTS!" (You can't just stick them under the dryer and move on and forget about them like out of sight, out of mind).

Let's talk to clients about Salon Etiquette. We will call this Salon Etiquette 1 on 1...LBVS. Have limited seating? Well don't allow your client to bring other people with them who are not being serviced. They shouldn't want to share that time anyway. This goes to all revenues. Unless the rest of your party has dealings with the company you are visiting; there is no need for them to be present. This could blow your deal. Have a sign on the entry door that says, "Due to limited seating, only people being serviced are welcome," along with the no public restrooms and no soliciting signs. I found that telling people that their party couldn't stay was found to be more offensive by the client.

Storytime! One day a client was referred to me by his mother, who worked with my sister (my biggest cheerleader, she is always selling me to people and I love and appreciate her for this) to get his dreadlocks tightened up and styled. This process takes about 2 hours, okay. The first time he came alone and loved his hair. The second time he came back he brought his girlfriend. The sign on the door let them know that no one could stay unless being serviced.

Now at the time I didn't know he brought his girlfriend. Because of the sign, she never made it inside. As time went by I was wondering why I hadn't seen the client for his dreadlocks to be tightened up. I was like, "What could have turned him off" because I always try to spoil people so that they do come back? I told my sister that I haven't seen so and so. She then told me she had talked to the young man's mother and the young man had told his mom that he was not coming back because his girlfriend was not welcome to stay unless she was getting a service. I was like, "WOW!" This is what turned him off?! I was appalled! End of story.

See, I thought that the client would appreciate this. I mean, I, the hairstylist, have an appointment with you, the client, not your BFF nor your cousin nor your significant other. I mean, this is our (client to stylist) time to share and get to know each other. This is when you get to ask me all your hair questions, so we can make sure you get the most out of the look you want. You want to learn how to maintain your hair; to get the best results. Teaching and educating are one of your services that can increase your revenue.

Clients like to know that you are not just taking their money but actually care about them. And that's a GOOD FEELING that will increase your chances of them returning for more. See, if you bring people along with you for your personal appointments it's a distraction from the experience. Distractions (like being on the phone, running in and out, coming to an appointment sick, needing too many bathroom breaks...the list goes on and on) can totally take away from the experience. Emergencies I can totally understand (of course), but too much moving around only makes completing the service complicated and it takes longer.

You want to be respectful of other's time. Time is the only thing people can't get back, so respect that. I mean, could you imagine having an interview for a job and the interviewee shows up with a friend or child? That's probably not going to work out and could totally jeopardize you getting that job. It's unacceptable, and I'm sure you learned this as a child. Like, using your time wisely. We have heard this from a kid to adulthood.

So, Stylist, when you put your client under the dryer make sure you continue to check on them. Reassure them that you are still available. This is comforting and makes them feel really appreciated. Now, you can use this down time whichever way you want. But, might I suggest not going to the mall! That's just not acceptable. Your client is paying for your time for you to be available for them, even if they are under the hair dryer.

What if, just WHAT IF, your client had a question? They could totally get turned off knowing that you were not available for their questions. This can jeopardize building that long-term relationship. If you have time in between meetings, calls or clients, it would be the more appropriate to:

1. Set up for the other half of your occurring appointment
2. Prepare for the next client.
3. Market your business.
4. Eat something (not too much or this can give you fatigue).

IT'S SHOWTIME Whewwwwheewww! The drying time has ended, and the client is headed back to the chair. (Here is a little habit that I do that may help you). I ask the client would they like a restroom break before I start the other half of the service. This gets everything out of the way, so you can execute the service with as less interruptions as possible, yet you are still catering to their needs (this makes people feel so good, something so small and so effortless can be so powerful).

While you are servicing your client, explain to them what you are doing (I found that clients really appreciate you taking the time to explain to them what you are doing; clients seem to love this; they want that personal connection with you) and how they can maintain the style (this shows that you really care about their needs). Rushing clients out the door (whether it's an interview, church, a haircut, a party entertainer you hired...whomever) it is rude and they may never return. Because you were short with them they may be offended. I know I hate being rushed at a restaurant.

No one likes to feel taken. Especially, when, they are spending money. I even suggest products for them to use. Providing the retail sale of the products used during their service will not only help them maintain healthy hair habits but also makes your job easier when they return. And it will also increase your numbers in sales. Now who doesn't want more money?

Well, finesse, patience and smiles seemed to always increase my tips. CHA-CHING BABY! When people are spending their hard-earned money with you, they expect you to cater to them. DO IT! They will appreciate all the tips and product knowledge you share. But, know that you are in charge of the tone you set. Everyone in the salon plays a part in setting the tone starting with the stylist. OH YES! It's all you at first. You applied for a job at a certain location because you liked something about that company. The same thing applies when you want to build a solid foundation in a relationship. It's that Law of Attraction (you know the things people do to make people gravitate to them).

TRUE STORY

I remember when I was about to get out of Cosmetology School. I heard of this girl I knew who had a salon. I knew that when I graduated and passed my State Boards test that it was where I wanted work. I had heard so many good things about this salon; from the work the owner did, to what a great location it was, to the clientele that came through the salon.

Needless to say, I was SOLD on the salon from just the stories alone. I had to go check it out for myself! It was everything I wanted in a salon. I had like a month to go before I graduated, but I kept showing up at the salon making sure the lady saved my station. I even went so far as to telling her which station I wanted. See, when you are serious about something and you really want it you must stay persistent and consistent. This shows respect.

I respect myself by making plans and securing the plans. If you want respect from others, then you must show them you mean business. And that's just what I was doing. All I wanted to do was show my skills. I wanted the owner to know that I was just as good as she was, fresh out of school. I was one year in and had smoked myself out. What does that mean?

Well, I made sure I worked so hard and mastered my skill. Finally, she recognized my work and gave me a shot. She was going on maternity leave and wanted me to take over her clients until she came back off maternity leave. Omg! I thought, ok here is my chance. I had watched this lady make hundreds of dollars a day, so I was more than excited for this opportunity. Since I was fresh out of school I could use the extra exposure. The exposure would bring me more opportunities, which then meant more money. I wanted to make the lady proud, so I went the extra mile for her clients. I was perky, fast, (cause this lady was known for speed) and I even took people that walked in without an appointment, and that was something that she just didn't do.

Her clients were SO HAPPY that they were able to come in and get almost the same service that their original hairstylist gave them, but an array of new hairstyles. See, I thought I was making her proud. Oh, but when she came back, some of her clients stayed with me. (I mean she was doing like over a dozen people a day, she was rolling in dough $$$).

So, now if the owner was busy, the clients would just ask me to service them, since I had proven myself and kept them happy and coming back for more. Well, the owner did not like that. In her eyes, I was flaunting my talent and trying to make her look bad. In the 48 Laws of Power it's says "he will not admit the truth, but he will find an excuse to rid himself of your presence." That is just what she did, so eventually I quit. I wouldn't let that change who, I am, so I left gracefully and proud. End of story.

I know that growth can sometimes be intimidating and shocking to some people. You must realize that you can inadvertently outshine a master simply by being you.

TRUE STORY

I remember working at a salon that I was quite pleased with. The lady had begged for me to come and work with her in her salon. She got a chance to see my work ethic twice, and she was so super impressed by the services that she witnessed me giving out. Not only to my clients but she saw how I interacted with the staff and their clients. She said she loved my spirit and I was COLD BLOODED with my hands and she was taking me from the salon where I currently worked...LBVS. So, when I left one salon I decided to go work with this salon.

The owner was all welcoming and caring....at first. She served snacks, educated her clients and staff on products, she had an open-door policy. She also had a sign on the door that said due to capacity of the salon that only people being serviced were allowed to stay. Sounds fine, Right?

Well it was, until one day the owner decided to get a dog. SHE got a dog. NOT me. NOT, my clients! .Shoot NOT even her clients! She brought that dog to work with her everyday just about. I mean it was just a puppy. Sounds harmless, right? WRONG! Not only did I find this disturbing, disrespectful and annoying, so did many of the clients.

When clients are coming to do business with YOU! That's just who they want to deal with. They do not want to be bothered with all of your personal situations. Now there is barely room for clients, but now there is a dog cage, dog toys, dog snacks, even a really nicely made dog bed.

See. When you make rules, you have to abide by the rules as well, or people can begin to lose respect for you. You cannot expect people to respect you if you disrespect yourself. Maybe she felt like the rules didn't apply to her because it was her salon. WRONG! Once you invite a staff into your company and set rules and sign contracts, they are now part of your business. So, you have to consider their needs as well.

A couple months after the dog arrived with no notice, I noticed I had lost a few clients. People would complain about the puppy. It was not house broken. It would jump up on my clients, eat people's food' poop and pee everywhere. The owner would even ask if we (the staff or clients) saw the mess, why didn't we just clean it up?

REALLY?! The lady would bully people into helping take care of her dog. Even, taking long breaks to walk the dog in between clients. Sometimes this would slow me down cause she would have the dryers tied up and walking the dog only made her clients drying time longer so

I would have to wait on dryers. Sometimes, she would leave the dog in the salon while she was gone for hours, while the puppy cried. Some of my clients actually told me to call them once I left this location, because they could no longer take the atmosphere. She didn't consider the salon's setting (atmosphere) over her own personal feelings.

When you are doing business, you must appeal to your clients and be aware of their feelings. Once you decide that your personal dealings are more important than your clients, they will feel this, and it could totally jeopardize your business. You have to practice what you preach if you want the respect you deserve or have workers work hard for you. She went back on her word and the staff and clients were reminded of this every time they walked up to the door and saw that DUE TO CAPACITY sign. And then walked in and saw that there was room for a whole dog but no room for the people who probably gave them the money to even get the service. This was rude and offensive. If you want to stay respected, then you have to stay respectful. Finish how you start!

Setting the Tone

Chapter 6

Atmosphere is EVERYTHING! If a person is having a bad day, all HELL could break loose. So, you want to provide a nice environment for you clients. Providing light snacks for clients puts them at ease if they have to wait on being serviced. I worked with a lady that would even bring home cooked food in just for her clients.

They actually loved the personal touches coming from her kitchen. They liked the feeling of knowing she thought of them outside of being behind the chair. She wanted to share her home away from the salon with them, and this was a nice gesture that meant a lot to the clients. Sometimes the clients would come in looking for food and making all these requests and she would politely shut them down yet giving them something for next time.

See, the owner would religiously bring snacks and/or food or wine, and clients would get accustomed to this. So, don't start something you can't finish because this could turn them off. I worked in a salon where a lady would provide non-slip footies to accommodate her clients. Knowing she had a lot of corporate women that wore dress shoes (heels) all day and would come religiously after work to get serviced, she knew they would want to take their shoes off. Nice huh?

One lady provided a charging station for all clients' electronic devices. (See this is how one stays in control while still making it about the clients and this makes them feel appreciated; seriously, talking about going the extra mile). I mean, having clients constantly wanting to charge their devices and get up to check the device while being charged only makes doing business a hassle.

I remember I used to see these little blue hospital shoe covers in the winter time piled up by the door when you entered the salon. I'm like ok who's are these when in first saw them. (See, if you have wooden flooring at your business or home or if you just mopped, you didn't want people messing up your floor, Right?) The owner of the salon told me that she asks that people put them over their shoes or removed their shoes when it snowed, (unless they wanted to replace the floor she would honestly joke) because the salt that people put down to melt ice can eat up a wooden flooring. This lady set the tone how she wanted it while still making it about the client.

[You have to know what pulling out all the stops and knowing when to stop, means.] If you do not set the tone, the client will set it for you (that makes doing your job hard). Just remember that all things are possible, and NO, the customer is not always right. No matter what a client asks for, be accommodating. Provide options for a professional decision.

When a client books an appointment with you, you know they have all these great ideas. You must hear them out. We know from experience that they just want what they want and have NO IDEA the work that has to go into creating that look. Looks pretty simple to them, and they want you to do it the way they say do it. See, this is when that saying "the customer is always right" ...is WRONG.

You know your job. they trust you doing your job, so why do they want to be the director? I don't know. But, I do know you cannot be like...”UH UHHHNNN honey that ain't even going to look right, or you ain't got enough hair for that, and umm well that's going to cost you this and that and so on and so forth.” “Child please” as my mom would say. If I had listened to every client that told me how to do my job, I wouldn't have a job. The client is the executive producer; the merely fund the idea. Stay the director and produce, but don't be rude, because they client can sense that, and it could totally jeopardize building a long-term relationship.

When a client wants to do business with you, most likely they saw your work and loved it, or they heard really good things about you (good manners) (pretty, poise and polite) and they were convinced and wanted to experience you for themselves. Either way it was something YOU did. SO, why when they come in do they want to be the director? I have no idea. No matter how far a customer goes, it is your job to stay professional. Question... If a client complains about a service, what do you do?

A. Give them a refund for the services or product.

B. Set a day and time for you to talk with the un satisfied client.

C. Tell them sorry no refunds.

True Story: I was working at this salon and by then I had had my license for over 12 years. One of my clients calls me and tells me she was at the laundromat and a young lady just loved her hair, so she gave the young lady my phone number. They continue talking. The young lady went into how she went to a braiding shop to get her hair braided and she was so unhappy, so she went back for them to correct what she was unhappy about.

The young lady goes on and on about how no one could give her what she wanted. So, of course my client went into sale mode for me.... I just love my clients. By the time my client was done talking about me, needless to say the young lady was SOLD on me and my services. The young lady is now at the salon to book an appointment. (Saying her hair was JACKED UP is an understatement) LBVS.

As we start our consultation I noticed she had all of these require-ments and restrictions. (she couldn't do it at this time, she had to be out by this time, she only wanted to use this type of hair, etc... etc..). I knew then that this was not the type of client that I was not interested in, but I stayed professional. I was trying to be so accommodating BUT, if a client comes in with all of these requirements, most likely it's going to be a problem. When she came in to get the service done, she had the type of hair that you use for a totally different type of procedure. (could you imagine cutting a watermelon with a butter knife). You need the correct tools to do the job is all I'm saying.

As a hair stylist I found it is easier for you and takes some of the responsibility off your client and they feel extra at ease if you purchase ALL the tools and product needed in completing a service, including hair, and include it into the price of the service. I found that clients actually get overwhelmed when they have to pick out hair extensions. They want you to do it all.

Back, to the story though. The young lady said that even though she knew that this was not the hair that is used for this particular procedure, this is the hair she wanted to use. I advised her to go get different hair because that was not the correct hair for the procedure she wanted. She did not care. She would risk the braids slipping out of her hair.

Well, you know what? I proceeded to do her hair the way SHE wanted it done. (This was my professional mistake. I just gave her control). I twisted the chair around so the young lady could see herself in the oversized wall mirror. "WOW I LOVE IT" she says...all smiling and swinging her hair from side to side. She then continued to say, "this is just what I wanted!" I was like, "I'm happy you are happy."

A couple of days went by and the young lady calls me up saying a couple of her braids slipped out (just like I said they would so why is she calling me like I didn't do my job?) Right? So, I told the young lady to come back in to the salon and I would reinstall the ones that slipped out FREE of charge. (Me being accommodating) When the young lady came in, it seemed as if she took the whole front section of her hair down, and that's not what we agreed upon, but, ok.

Now, I am being over accommodating to the client and this could be a really bad move sometimes. Although you are in the business of making clients happy, and feel good about themselves don't lose your control (temper). When the young lady came back in she told me what SHE wanted again. Still knowing the correct procedure, she insisted I do it her way.

So, that is what I did. I braided the client's hair over, giving her EXACTLY what she asked for. Again, she left the salon pleased. Further into the week that same client pops up at the salon with no appointment, demanding that she speaks with me! The young lady was informed that I was booked for the day and when I was free to speak with her I would give a call. But, that was not good enough for the client.

She barged pass the reception area and stormed up to my chair (that was occupied by another client) and demanded I speak with her right now. She was irate! The young lady stood right over me and the client in the chair and got loud and belligerent. At this point I didn't know what to do?

1. **Do I walk away from the client in the chair and address the situation? 2. Do I continue working as if the irate client is not there and call security? I didn't want to risk losing two clients and the way I would handle this would determine just that.**

The test of good manners is to be able to be able to put up pleasantly with bad ones.

-Wendell Willkie

My client in the chair turned around and looked at the lady as if she was a crazy person. Now, if I don't handle this situation correctly not only could I lose the unsatisfied client (which I wouldn't miss if this is how they act) and the person in the chair could be so shocked that they don't return, time, for some finesse.

The salon I was working in at the time had a strict policy against people walking freely through the salon if not being serviced, so how she got past the front desk was puzzling to me. I was appalled, because I rarely got complaints, especially since I explained the procedure and what would happen and over compensated her. This was going to stop...NOW.

Before I knew it, I had stopped working on the client in the chair and was now facing the irate client, rolling my eyes, sucking my teeth and going to give her a piece of my mind. I had totally shut down. She had gotten me. Once you lose control you just don't know what your next move may be, but I am pretty sure it will be self-destruction at its best. That's when the salon staff noticed and stepped in, escorting the young lady out of the salon. End of story.... or is it? My son would say.

You Are the Roux

"When we are no longer able to change a situation, we are challenged to change ourselves."

-Victor E. Frankl

Chapter 7

I decided this when I was a little girl. Being the one that got called names (like Bucky Beaver because my teeth protruded as I was a thumb sucker, or bald head monkey because my hair was so short and kinky, or I have an even better one...how about alligator woman? Because my skin was scaly... not ashy...scaly, big difference) and teased until I cried myself all the way back home. I knew that I never wanted to make people feel rejected, especially from feeling ugly. That's a very insecure place. I decided that I would treat people the way I wanted to be treated, and maybe they would treat me the same. But when something like, good manners, kindness, and consideration of other's feelings backfires on you, this can be shocking and hurtful. Especially, when you do all this and still get fired. Well, kind of fired.

I work for myself, so I can't really get fired, but these clients employ me so if they don't return, then I guess I KIND OF get fired (or that one time I was asked to leave this lady's salon). When I came to work at this salon the owner was all over me. Hyping me up, telling me I was like the ROUX to her Gumbo. Oh! Now, that made me so very proud. I had never worked in a salon full of so many women and they were doing services I wasn't, so I was a bit intimidated when I got there. But when the owner called ME the Roux to her Gumbo, honey my mind was now at ease. Now if anyone knows about Gumbo, you know that this is a very serious southern dish. You don't go messing around making this dish unless you really know what you are doing. That Roux can be tricky. Oh baby, the Roux is what makes Gumbo, Gumbo.

The Roux is the most important ingredient! It has to be thick; not thin like soup. So, when she said this to me I was so very proud and geeked up. I had to show her that I could be just that. I wanted to show her I am alllll that. I would take the towels home and wash them if they got piled up. I was just about the first person to open the salon. I always smiled and looked good and smelled good. I mean I was so polite and poised that other stylist's clients loved me and brought new business, gifts, and wanted to take selfies with me. I mean I thought I was really happy, but this became draining. No one else was going the extra mile and that bothered me. MESSAGE!

Now it's been 2 years in the salon and I my Roux must have gotten thin honey because one day the owner asked to speak with me and I was asked to leave the salon. I was appalled. The nerve of this lady I thought after all I had done and had taken. The owner's reason was she said she had gotten A complaint about me and she couldn't have that type of attention on her shop's name. Then she goes on to say that I just don't seem happy at work anymore. LMFAO, well I wasn't! Ha! So she kind of fired me, but only at the end of the day after I had opened up her salon, took calls, wrote out messages and put them on sticky notes and put them on the staffs stations, greeted other stylists' clients that hadn't arrived yet, including the owner's (who always seemed to be running late; cute but late) and made coffee and served it as well.

So, when she asked me to leave I was really upset, but I couldn't show it. See, I had already done enough abuse to myself. I just sat there pretty, poised and polite like I do and listened, kind of condescendingly listened...if you want to be honest. I smiled and nodded and minded my manners. Seems to me she didn't have a solid reason for firing me and she was reaching for anything. She then informed me that the client that "wanted what she wanted" you know the "irate client with the braids" had called and was very upset and she just couldn't have that type of attention on her salon's name.

One complaint! That just goes to show you no matter how much good you do, you do one wrong thing and that's what people will judge you on. Sad! But true. Nawl! This couldn't be the reason I thought to myself. But I was ok with whatever her reasons were because it was her establishment. But she put some things on my mind, so I began to self-reflect, because I know it had to be something else. Like Louis XIV said in the 48 Laws of Power... You can outshine the master by your charm and grace instead of your skill. See, the owner was so impressed by my skills, but we had a difference in our target audience, so she never seemed intimidated by my work, but she seemed intimidated by my work ethic. So that very thing that got me hired, eventually got me fired. That must be some nasty Gumbo now, huh?

Sometimes the right kind of NO is better than the wrong kind of yes....

See, I had to take responsibility for myself and my own actions of getting myself fired. I quit, not literally, but mentally I had given up. I had checked out mentally. I started to have "Poor Salon Etiquette" if you will. My mannerisms changed, which only made my work harder and I became very unhappy. In my own situation, that I had total control over, so why would I put myself in this place? Oh, maybe because it was so easy. Anything, easy is not worth having.

If you do what is easy, your life will be hard. But, if you do what is hard, your life will be easy.

-Les Brown

It is so very easy to fall into temptation and become complacent. Working hard towards your goals (whatever those may be) is constant hard work. It will have you tired and doubtful, looking at other people lives. Wondering how they are doing it? WRONG MOVE! If you rely on other to get you to your happy place, you will constantly be disappointed. You will continue to keep starting over which can be frustrating discouraging and usually leads to self-destruction…eventually.

So, yes. It's ME. ME. ME. ME, and I had to own it all. You know, "take some responsibility." See, you are in control of your presence, and the people you are around, feed off of your energy. It was obvious that I was unhappy, although I still did my job, part of the owner's job and the receptionist…sheesh I was rolling. Huh? Maybe the owner noticed my posture was different, maybe I was a little slouched over instead of sitting straight up, walking tall and confident and perky like when I first walked in for the position. Showing, "HI! I'm happy to be here honey!" It could be the way I spoke when interacting with the other staff members.

I was being kind of short now (yes, no, maybe, I don't know). That definitely lets one know you are not here for it, ok, meaning I am here to do my job and that's it. Well, that can be kind of rude. Maybe it was the way I now took my lunch, I mean I still sat in the salon break room and ate, so what's the deal? Well the deal is, now, I'm not engaging in the staff's conversations in the break room. I kind of just ate in silence and went back to work. When at first, I ate, talked, laughed, shared my food, all that happy stuff. Maybe it's the expression on my face as I worked, even though I was doing a job that made me happy, I was unhappy doing it. If, that even makes any sense.

You know when you go to a salon or barbershop and everyone is usually smiling and talking with one another and fraternizing with the customers? Well, I had totally stopped that, I mean you could tell I was unhappy. People began to ask me what was wrong, was I ok? I would give a fake smile and fake answer to assure them I'm perfectly fine (Fucked-up Irritated Negative Emotional wreck). So, with that being said, me getting fired could have been an array of things, and that's why there was no specific reason. I do thank her today for releasing me of my own toxic energy. I was sabotaging myself.

[See, confidence, standing, straight upward, walking tall, smiling, good hygiene, which I still had...lol...caring and sharing, being kind and nice and all the gory goodness of wooing and loving they neighboring in between]. Well, I found out it makes living life much easier and it makes the world a better place through one's eyes.

You don't build a business - you build people and then the people build the business.

If you want to increase your money and power, it all comes from Respect. To get to the money, you need the power. To keep the power you need the respect. And respect starts with self. Self-respect is something that no one can take from you. Once we lose that Self-Respect it's hard to find respect for the things or people around us. This can be self-destructive. Treat people like people and not numbers. I know this being nice and polite and all smiling is hard to do sometimes. But, I'm telling you from experience that Good Manners makes life easier and more staid-saying.

Just try it. Practice some of these tips I gave you and watch how people begin to gravitate to you. They will want to be involved in whatever it is positive that you want to do. You want to get the deal, seal the deal and then secure the deal. Rather it is for a job or for building up your family, especially families. There are so many broken homes right now because of the cracks (disrespect) in the foundation (self-respect) that are being laid for our future generations. Keep in mind what you did to get the deal because that is how you maintain the deal.

Your, charm your, mannerism. It is in you. It always has been in you. You are the key to your success. Tap into your inner you. Yes I know it can be a daring, scary, lonely place, to face yourself and to face that you have been that very person holding you back. It is so AWAKENING! Don't be afraid of yourself. WAKE UP IN THERE!

Being pretty, poised and polite, well that's just good manners. Remember, you can't win them all, but the key is to build long lasting relationships and what better way to start than with self-respect and good manners. Trust it. It will bring you good fortune and friends.

"You can have it all, just not all at once. The biggest secret is that there is no secret. Whatever your goal, you can get there if you're willing to work. Go ahead fall down, the world looks different from the ground."

-Oprah Winfrey